Around the world in

32 PULL-OUT PRINTS

DAVID DORAN

For Izzy,
for all the cities we've seen together
and all the ones we're yet to.

1 3 5 7 9 10 8 6 4 2

Virgin Books, an imprint of Ebury Publishing,
20 Vauxhall Bridge Road,
London SW1V 2SA

Virgin Books is part of the Penguin Random House group of companies
whose addresses can be found at global.penguinrandomhouse.com

Penguin
Random House
UK

First published by Virgin Books in 2017

www.penguin.co.uk

A CIP catalogue record for this book is available from the British Library

ISBN 9780753545409

Design by Maru Studio

Printed and bound in China by Toppan Leefung

Penguin Random House is committed to a sustainable
future for our business, our readers and our planet.
This book is made from Forest Stewardship Council®
certified paper.

is for AMSTERDAM

is for AMSTERDAM

There are 165 canals weaving their way throughout the busy city of Amsterdam, which adds up to nearly 60 miles worth of waterways. To help its many tourists and cyclists travel around, there are nearly 1,500 bridges.

Many of Amsterdam's inhabitants live in houseboats on the canals, with more than 3,000 moored up around the city.

is for BARCELONA

is for BARCELONA

Designed by the architect Antoni Gaudí in the early twentieth century, Park Güell is one of the most celebrated spots in Barcelona. Inspired by natural forms, the park is a twisting series of curved benches, archways and steps covered in brightly coloured mosaic tiles.

It is said that Gaudi asked his builders to test the comfort of each bench as it was made, to ensure that the visitors to the park would be able to fully relax and enjoy their time there.

is for CAIRO

is for CAIRO

*There are over a hundred pyramids in Egypt, and
the three most famous of them stand in Giza Necropolis,
on the outskirts of Cairo.*

*The Great Pyramid of Giza, which is said to have needed
up to 200,000 people to build, held the record for the
tallest man-made structure for over 3,800 years.*

is for DUBAI

is for DUBAI

Dubai is the fastest-growing city in the world.
In 1968 it was recorded that there were only 13 cars
in the entire city, but it is now so densely populated
and congested with traffic that double-decker roads
have been built to ease the problem.

The ever-changing and unique skyline of Dubai is home
to the striking Burj Al Arab. Inspired by the sails
of a ship, it is the third-tallest hotel in the world
and once claimed to be the only seven-star
hotel in existence.

is for EDINBURGH

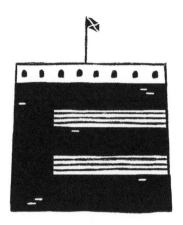

is for EDINBURGH

*Edinburgh Castle is built on the site of an extinct volcano
and is one of the best-defended fortresses in Scottish
history. The Castle is full of many hidden staircases
and secret passageways, which enabled its royal
residents to sneak between rooms.*

*In the Great Hall, there is a small window above
the large main fireplace known as the 'Laird's Lug'
(Lord's Ear), which enabled eavesdropping
on conversations in the rooms below.*

is for FRANKFURT

is for FRANKFURT

The first printed books were sold in Frankfurt's bustling markets from as early as the fifteenth century, and by the sixteenth and seventeenth centuries the city had become the hub of book distribution across Europe.

Nowadays, the Frankfurt Book Fair is acknowledged to be the world's largest, attracting a vast global audience of book-publishing professionals and more than a quarter of a million visitors each year.

is for GUATEMALA CITY

is for GUATEMALA CITY

Guatemala City has four large volcanoes towering above it, two of which are currently active.

The country's currency is the Guatemalan quetzal, named after the resplendent national bird which features on the flag. In ancient Mayan times, the elegant and colourful tail feathers of this bird were used as currency.

is for HONOLULU

is for HONOLULU

Honolulu, which means 'sheltered harbour', is Hawaii's
capital city. It is located on the island of Oahu,
which has some of the oldest mountain ranges
in the world and is loved for its tropical
climate and spectacular beaches.

Honolulu upholds some unusual laws —
it is illegal to annoy a bird there
in a public park.

is for ISTANBUL

is for ISTANBUL

Istanbul is located on two continents, Europe and Asia, making it a transcontinental city.

The huge dome atop one of Istanbul's most famous landmarks, Hagia Sophia, is only slightly smaller than the Pantheon in Rome. The dome is so big that, when it was put in place, the walls of the church began to lean outward.

is for JERUSALEM

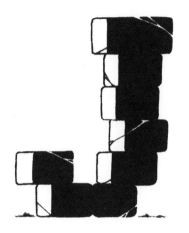

is for JERUSALEM

The ancient and holy city of Jerusalem, meaning
'City of Peace', is a place of pilgrimage for
numerous religious groups.

The famous Western Wall, otherwise known as the
'Wailing Wall', has over a million pieces of paper placed
between the cracks in the bricks, each with a prayer on,
every year. Twice a year, the Rabbi of the Western Wall
and his assistants collect and bury them in the
Jewish cemetery on the Mount of Olives.

is for KIEV

is for **KIEV**

*The monument in the centre of Maidan Nezalezhnosti,
or 'Independence Square', depicts Berehynia, a goddess
in Slavic mythology. It was built in 2001 to celebrate
Ukraine's independence. Independence Square has been
renamed at least eight times throughout Ukraine's
tumultuous political history.*

is for LONDON

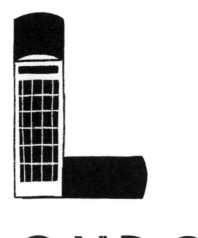

is for LONDON

The Houses of Parliament, officially known as the Palace of Westminster, were built next to the River Thames on the site of the medieval royal palace. Anyone who dies inside the Houses of Parliament is entitled to a state funeral.

is for LOS ANGELES

is for LOS ANGELES

According to an early map, Los Angeles was originally known as 'El Pueblo de la Reyna de los Angeles' (The town of the Queen of the Angels). Over time, the name has been shortened to 'The Angels'.

Los Angeles' iconic Hollywood sign originally said 'Hollywoodland', and was installed as an illuminated advertisement for a real-estate development of the same name.

is for MOSCOW

is for MOSCOW

The Kremlin, which means 'fortress inside a city',
is a fortified area within Moscow that contains five
palaces, four cathedrals and some of the most ornate
and unique architecture in the world.

Within the grounds of the Kremlin, visitors can view
the Tsar Bell, the largest in the world, which has
never been rung because it was damaged
during construction.

is for NASHVILLE

is for NASHVILLE

*World famous for its music scene, some of the most
celebrated pieces of music in modern history have been
recorded in the city of Nashville. During the recording
of an Elvis Presley Christmas album in the middle of
July, Christmas lights were strung up in RCA's Historic
Studio B to help Presley get into a festive mood.
They still hang there to this day.*

is for NEW YORK

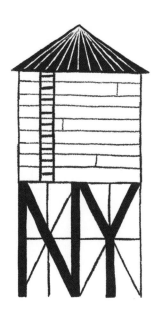

is for NEW YORK

Many people think the water towers peppering
New York's skyline are disused, but they actually provide
drinking and bathing water to the tenants of the
city's many high-rise buildings.

Manhattan's Flatiron building is known for its
unusual wedge shape. The more important you are
in the Flatiron Building, the nearer your office is
to the end of the wedge.

is for OSLO

is for OSLO

The people of Oslo have donated the Trafalgar Square Christmas tree in London every year since 1947, in gratitude to the people of Great Britain for their assistance during the Second World War.

The spectacular Norway spruce is selected months or even years prior to cutting based on its symmetrical form and strong colour, and is usually 50 to 60 years old by the time it is felled. It is cut in a ceremony attended by the Lord Mayor of Westminster, the British Ambassador to Norway and the Mayor of Oslo and shipped across the sea to the UK.

is for PARIS

is for PARIS

Place des Vosges, home to the city's classic wrought-iron lampposts and decadent architectural design, is the oldest planned square in Paris. It was built by King Henri IV and opened in 1612.

The most famous piece of architecture in Paris, the Eiffel Tower, which weighs approximately 10,000 tonnes, can grow up to 15 centimetres in the sun.

is for QUÉBEC CITY

is for QUÉBEC CITY

Québec City boasts the world's most photographed hotel, Le Château Frontenac. Set near the bank of Québec's picturesque St Lawrence River, the elegant hotel has a fairy-tale castle façade and attracts visitors from around the world, including monarchs and world leaders.

is for REYKJAVIK

is for REYKJAVIK

During the summer, Reykjavik gets almost 24 hours of daylight, while during the winter there can be as little as 4 hours of light in a day.

Despite the extreme climate of the city, it is extremely popular and visited by thousands of tourists each year.

In 1924, dogs were banned from Reykjavik to prevent the spread of diseases. The ban was lifted in 2006, but there is still a noticeably higher ratio of cats to dogs on the streets.

is for RIO DE JANEIRO

is for RIO DE JANEIRO

Rio de Janeiro means 'River of January', and it is said to have been named by a group of explorers in the sixteenth century who mistakenly thought the main bay area, now Guanabara Bay, was actually the mouth of a river.

Around 11 million of the nearly 200 million residents of Brazil live in the infamous favelas, the densely built up slum areas, many of which sprawl across Rio's steep slopes.

is for SYDNEY

is for SYDNEY

Nearly 600 species of fish have been recorded in Sydney
Harbour, which is more than double the number
you would find off the coast of the whole of
the United Kingdom.

Sitting prominently on the edge of the harbour
and inspired by the sails of the many boats, the
famous Sydney Opera House was completed ten
years past its deadline and surpassed its original
costing of AUS $7 million, costing over
AUS $100 million in the end.

is for SAN FRANCISCO

is for SAN FRANCISCO

The iconic Golden Gate Bridge was never meant to be the International Orange colour that it is so known for now. The Navy wanted it to be painted yellow and black, but the architect chose the distinctive orange as it blended well with the warm colours of surrounding land masses.

Strangely, the Chinese fortune cookie is often credited as being invented in San Francisco – by a Japanese man.

is for TOKYO

is for TOKYO

The culture of the geisha, which translates as 'artist',
originated in Japan.

A geisha's formal kimono can take up to three years to
create. It is made from one single length of fabric reaching
12 metres long, and none of the material is wasted.
Despite the length of time they take to make,
a geisha will usually choose to wear her
kimono only once.

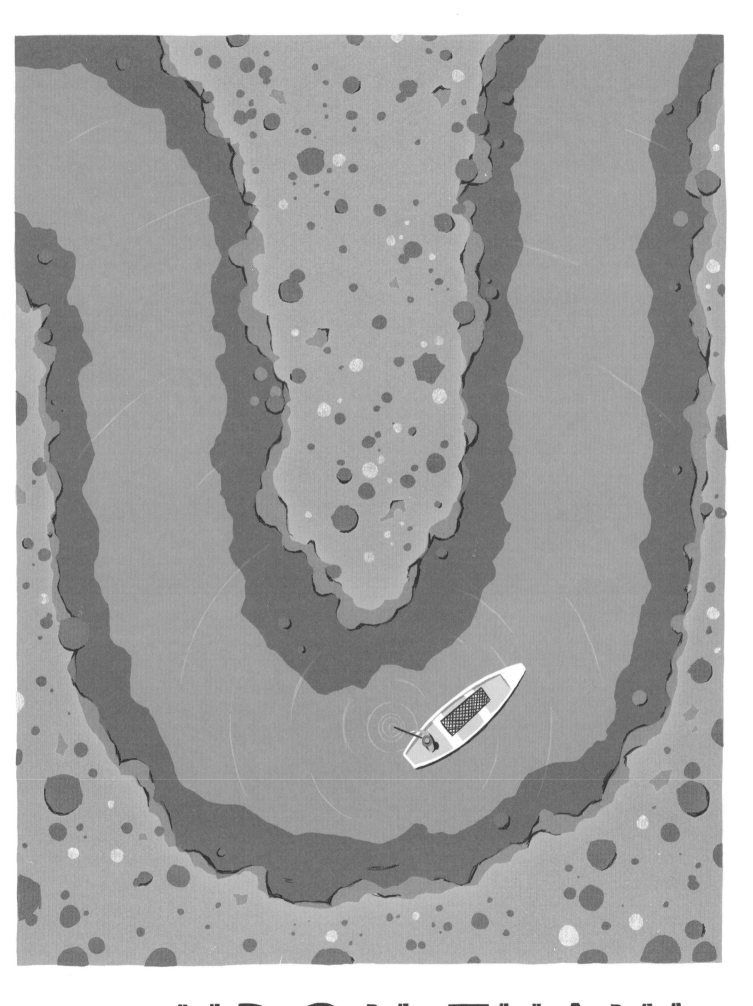

is for UDON THANI

is for UDON THANI

Udon Thani is a city in Thailand near to the Talay Bua Daeng, – 'The Red Lotus Sea' – home to over a million vibrant-crimson water lilies.

Visitors can boat through the lake, which is thick with beautiful flowers and best viewed in full bloom during the months of January and February.

is for VENICE

is for VENICE

Being a gondolier is a noble and highly respected profession in Venice, and only three or four gondolier licences are granted each year. To become a gondolier over 400 hours of training are required, which include mastering very specific rowing techniques and learning a foreign language. Venice licensed its first female gondolier in 2010.

is for WARSAW

is for WARSAW

The beautiful Old Town in the heart of Warsaw is
famed for its ornate architecture. However, the city was
repeatedly and heavily attacked during the Second World
War, destroying much of the city, which means that some
of the Old Town is less than 40 years old.

It was built using as much of the original brick rubble
as possible with the intricate design closely
replicating the original.

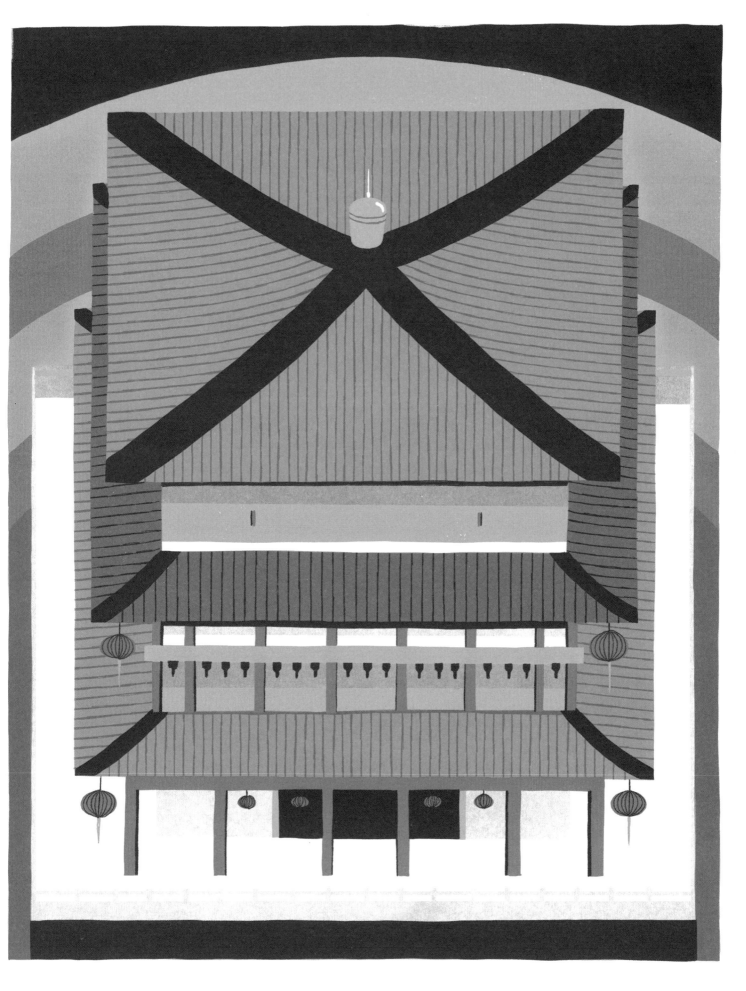

is for XI'AN

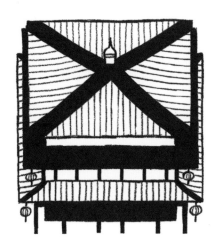

is for XI'AN

Xi'an is one of the Four Great Ancient Capitals of China,
with a rich history during many of the country's longest-
serving dynasties. Xi'an is famous for the splendid
Terracotta Army, which was found inside the tomb
of the first Chinese emperor Qin Shi Huang.

The collection comprises a staggering
8,000 soldiers, with 130 chariots, 520 horses
and 150 cavalry horses.

is for YANGON

is for YANGON

Over 2,500 years old, the Shwedagon Pagoda dominates
the skyline in Yangon, Myanmar (formerly Burma),
and is one of the world's most revered Buddhist shrines.

The vast tower is covered in real gold, and at the very tip
the 'umbrella crown' is coated in 5,448 diamonds
and 2,317 rubies.

is for ZURICH

is for ZURICH

Zurich is renowned for its high quality of life and booming economy, but it also upholds some unique practices. The Swiss government introduced strict laws to educate on animal rights and guarantee that all pets were well looked after, including one which demands that all 'social' animals, such as budgerigars, goldfish and guinea pigs, must be kept in pairs or larger groups to ensure that they won't get lonely.